Grammar

Grammar

Section 1 — Word Types

Page 2 — Nouns

1. You should have underlined: **Brazil, monkey, girl, pencil, April, Emma.**

2. Common nouns: **game, tree, dog, money, house, book**
   Proper nouns: **London, Daniel, December, Tuesday, Rachel, America**

Page 3 — Adjectives

1. You should have underlined: **happy, quiet, purple, small, famous, clever, silly.**

2. Any suitable adjectives. Examples:
   the **confused** bear, the **brown** bear
   the **happy** man, the **relaxed** man
   the **scared** penguin, the **running** penguin
   the **huge** carrot, the **big** carrot

Pages 4 and 5 — Articles

1. Yesterday we saw **an** alligator.
   Melanie has **a** TV in her room.
   I would like **a** hamburger.
   Here's **an** apple.

2. There's **an** orange in the fruit bowl.
   My sister has got **a** boyfriend.
   A cat has just run through the garden.
   If it snows, we could build **an** igloo.

3. Olga saw **an** elephant on the way to school.
   There was **a** spider in the bath.
   The play was **a** disaster.
   An eagle flew over the houses.

4. We went to a café and Thomas ordered **a** drink.
   I would really like to go on **the** London Eye.
   Matthias and Isabel had **a** great time in Italy.
   He would like to know **the** truth.
   Mark says this book is **the** best one he's ever read.
   Michelle really needs **a** good night's sleep.
   The view from our bedroom window is wonderful.

5. Harriet was excited about her trip to **the** Eiffel Tower.
   When it's hot, we go out for **an** ice cream.
   Mum makes the best pancakes in **the** world.
   My computer has broken, so I need **a** new one.
   An afternoon walk through the park is a lovely idea.

Pages 6 and 7 — Verbs

1. You should have circled: **eat, be, see, talk, write, run, sit.**

2. Jenny and Joe **go** to the cinema on Fridays.
   He **has** a motorbike, a car and a van.
   The supporters **are** happy with the referee's decision.
   I **do** my homework as soon as I **get** home.
   Susie often **flies** to Germany to **see** her friends.

3. Heather **enjoys** playing tennis at the weekend.
   The children **walk** to school every day.
   Craig and Will **take** the train to work.
   She **hates** doing the washing-up.
   Daniel usually **meets** his friends in the park.

4. Ronnie **annoys** his sister by pulling her hair.
   Our dog **chases** the cat around the garden.
   A ghost **lives** in the castle.
   Mum and Dad **prepare** the dinner.

5. **play, cut**

Pages 8 and 9 — Adverbs

1. You should have underlined: **always, slowly, gently, next, then.**

2. The guests will arrive **soon**.
   The dog **playfully** licked my nose.
   He **rarely** goes to London.
   The children **greedily** ate the chocolate.
   Ivy **always** drives Mike to the shops.
   Maya **accidentally** fell and grazed her arm.

3. It's our turn **next**.
   Jonathan doesn't **often** complain.
   Lila **quickly** ran to the door.
   Shops are **usually** open every Monday.
   Calvin **quietly** sneaked past the house.
   We **busily** sorted through our things.
   Violet is **normally** late for school.
   The pupil **rudely** interrupted the teacher.

4. I wish it was always open, but **sometimes** it's closed.
   Linda **carefully** wrapped the presents.
   We never run out — our milk is delivered **daily**.
   Gary ate a lot — **afterwards** he felt really full.
   There wasn't room inside, so I had to wait **outside**.
   My brother's lazy — he **never** helps us.

Section 2 — Clauses and Phrases

Pages 10 and 11 — Clauses

1. Main clauses: **I love chips, they told lies, he plays hockey, it's dark, she's happy now**
   Subordinate clauses: **until they arrive, when it's over, while eating cheese, if you're coming, before the bell rang**

2. William drives to work <u>when it rains</u>.
   The girls keep the light on <u>because they're afraid of the dark</u>.
   <u>After she had played tennis</u>, Jean went out for dinner.
   <u>If the water rises any further</u>, we'll have to get help.

3. <u>The children were soaking wet</u> because it was raining outside.
   <u>I'll go swimming</u> while Timothy goes out for a run.
   Before we go out to play, <u>we need to tidy up</u>.
   <u>We couldn't see the stars</u> until the sun had gone down.
   If you do that again, <u>I won't play with you any more</u>.

Grammar

4. He enjoys watching cartoons while eating popcorn.
   I had a pudding after my main meal.
   Jane will play tennis if it stops raining.
   Rupert can't go to school until he's feeling better.
   The musicians practised before the concert.

5. Any suitable main clauses.
   Examples:
   Before we had dinner, **we played a game of cards**.
   While Chris plays the piano, **Charlie sings along**.
   When Mum arrived, **we all hid under the bed**.

Page 12 — Phrases

1. You should have ticked: **far too early**, **very difficult**, **really funny**, **before midnight**.

2. Any suitable phrases.
   Examples:
   Peter jumped **on the trampoline**.
   The teacher shouted **at the pupils**.
   Rabbits are **popular pets**.

Page 13 — Noun Phrases

1. You should have circled: **blue shoes**, **cuddly hamsters**, **those amazing colours**, **chocolate muffins**, **lazy elephants**, **all of the teachers**.
   The nouns are: **shoes**, **hamsters**, **colours**, **muffins**, **elephants**, **teachers**.

2. You should have circled: **monster**, **sofa**, **socks**, **houses**.

Pages 14 and 15 — Mixed Sentence Practice

1. Clauses: **let's go for a bike ride**, **sandwiches are nice**, **I like reading**.
   Phrases: **up the mountain**, **really tall men with red hair**, **a fun game**.

2. You should have circled: **every Wednesday**, **the deep, blue sea**, **a very muddy path**.

3. her shiny new bike: **noun phrase**
   After the sun had set: **subordinate clause**
   in the dark: **phrase**
   I cut the whole loaf of bread in half: **main clause**
   on a plate: **phrase**

4. Any suitable answers.
   Examples:
   I enjoyed playing football today **because we won the match**.
   He saw **the big pink teddy bear**, but he didn't like it.
   Time passes **very quickly** when you're having fun.

Section 3 — Sentences

Page 16 — Statements and Questions

1. Why is he angry? — question
   What's the time? — question
   I work in a bakery. — statement
   I am so hungry. — statement
   It is a windy day. — statement

How old are you? — question
When will you be back? — question
My mum's name is Kathy. — statement

2. Are they hungry?
   Are you fast?
   Am I outside?
   Is he alright?
   Are we downstairs?

Page 17 — Commands and Exclamations

1. Finish your vegetables. — C
   What a huge whale that was! — E
   How terrible that cake was! — E
   What a brilliant play we saw! — E
   How funny you are! — E
   What a day I've had! — E
   Fasten your seatbelts. — C
   How clever she is! — E
   Fill the pan with water. — C
   Share your sweets. — C

2. Commands:
   Hold the tray.
   Stop the car.
   Exclamations:
   How fun that was!
   What a clever baby he is!

Section 4 — Conjunctions and Prepositions

Pages 18 and 19 — Conjunctions with Main Clauses

1. You should have circled: **so**, **nor**, **and**, **but**, **for**, **yet**, **or**

2. You should have underlined these words:
   Leo is going on holiday, <u>so</u> he needs to pack his suitcase.
   I want to play outside, <u>but</u> it's raining.
   We visited Grandad, <u>and</u> we gave him his birthday present.
   Tomek doesn't like sausages, <u>nor</u> does he like mashed potato.
   Daisy can't bake cakes, <u>yet</u> she can bake very good biscuits.
   Mr Davies is flying to France, <u>for</u> it's quicker than driving.

3. I want to play chess, **and** Rosie wants to play too.
   The zoo was closed, **so** (or **but**) we went to the museum.
   They can have ice cream, **or** (or **and**) they can have fruit salad.
   The fields were flooded, **for** it had rained a lot.
   I don't like tomatoes, **but** I do like tomato ketchup.

4. I was late, **so** I ran to school.
   I can't play the piano, **but** I can play the flute.
   We could go out, **or** we could stay in.
   Julia can ride a bike, **and** she can ride a horse.

CGP

KS2 English
Targeted Answer Book

CGP
– books
like no others!

CGP

Year 3

Grammar • Punctuation • Spelling

Contents

Grammar

Punctuation

Spelling

Published by CGP

ISBN: 978 1 78294 150 7

www.cgpbooks.co.uk
Clipart from Corel®
Printed by Elanders Ltd, Newcastle upon Tyne.
Based on the classic CGP style created by Richard Parsons.

Text, design, layout and original illustrations © Coordination Group Publications Ltd. (CGP) 2014

Grammar

Pages 20 and 21 — Conjunctions with Subordinate Clauses

1. You should have underlined these words:
   <u>Before</u> we go to America, we need to get some dollars.
   I think we should play tennis <u>if</u> the wind calms down.
   Lily crossed things off the list <u>as</u> her mum did the shopping.
   <u>After</u> he finished his main course, Lee ordered a dessert.

2. You should have circled: **because, when, Before, although, If**

3. The teacher told us off **because** we were running indoors.
   Let's get some petrol **before** we completely run out.
   We had to unpack **after** we came back from camp.
   I wouldn't eat a worm **even if** you paid me to do it.
   I'm good at maths **while** Drew is better at English.

4. Any suitable endings.
   Examples:
   We usually play outside because **it's nice to get some fresh air**.
   Colin never feels very well after **eating too much**.
   Mum and Dad were pleased when **the plumber came**.
   The football match will be cancelled if **the pitch is too wet**.

Pages 22 and 23 — Prepositions

1. You should have circled: **under, into, in, on, over, to, above**.

2. The cat is **on** the bed.
   The bag is **next to** (or **beside** or **by**) the bed.
   The shoes are **under** (or **beneath**) the bed.
   The boy is sitting **at** the table.
   The lamp is **on** the table.
   The mouse is **under** (or **beneath**) the table.

3. Mr Gibson burst **into** the classroom. — **where**
   I brush my teeth **before** bedtime. — **when**
   A mouse ran **past** my foot. — **where**
   Grandpa fell asleep **during** the film. — **when**
   They stayed in **because of** the storm. — **why**

4. The Channel Tunnel goes **under** the sea.
   Tom's parrot flew **out of** the window and into the garden.
   It's a long journey **to** Scotland from London.
   It was too late to learn my lines **after** the show.
   I will meet you in front of the gate **in** 10 minutes.

5. Any sentence that uses a preposition correctly.
   Example:
   The squirrel jumped **over the fallen tree**.

Section 5 — Verb Tenses

Pages 24 and 25 — Present Tense and Past Tense

1. Past tense: stayed, stared, told, bought, spoke, played
   Present tense: go, relax, run, jump, are

2.

Present Tense	Past Tense		Present Tense	Past Tense
I behave	I behaved		I talk	I talked
I offer	I offered		I enjoy	I enjoyed
I work	I worked		I need	I needed
I ask	I asked		I live	I lived
I hope	I hoped		I open	I opened

3. Harvey visited me.
   We tore it up.
   Alisha talked a lot.
   Jenny fell over.
   Ben packed his bag.
   I took the register.

4. Across: 1: broke
   2: ate
   3: threw
   4: read
   5: danced
   Down: 1: beat
   2: froze
   3: wore
   4: dried

Pages 26 and 27 — Using 'ing' verbs in the Present

1. You should have ticked these sentences and underlined these words:
   The cat <u>is</u> <u>sleeping</u> on the rug.
   The church bells <u>are</u> <u>ringing</u>.
   Mrs Taylor <u>is</u> <u>speaking</u> to Miss Jones.

2. The children **are** laugh**ing** at Mr Burgess.
   My dad **is** pretend**ing** he's forgotten Mum's birthday.
   Janice **is** watch**ing** the pop band 'Give This' in concert.
   They **are** walk**ing** from Land's End to John o' Groats.
   Glenn and Scott **are** show**ing** Lisa around the town.

3. My sister is **racing** around the track.
   I am **leaving** the party at 8 o'clock.
   Jason's popcorn is **popping** in the pan.
   Dad is **taking** our dog for a walk.
   We are **trying** to find our way home.
   My aunt is **mopping** the kitchen floor.

4. A blackbird is tapping at the window.
   We are driving to Cardiff.
   I am inviting friends to my party.

Page 28 — Using 'ing' verbs in the Past

1. Harry **was playing** tennis outside.
   They **were making** paper planes.
   I **was dropping** Kyle off at home.
   She **was cleaning** her bedroom.
   We **were listening** to music.

2. I was helping Jake.
   David and Bob were chasing Marcus.
   We were putting up pictures.

Punctuation

Pages 29 to 31 — Past Tense with 'have'

1. You should have underlined these sentences:
Jim has followed me.
She has arrived.
Jude has explained it.
I have scratched my glasses.
Sue has talked to Phil.

2. Ronnie has arranged the furniture.
I have finished my homework.
George has married Victoria.
We have painted the walls.

3. You should have circled these words:
forgotten
come
risen
stolen
drunk

4. The wolf **has blown** the house down.
Bob **has thanked** everyone.
We **have shown** them our idea.
My sister **has given** me her clothes.
They **have kept** the money safe.
We **have enjoyed** the holiday.
I **have broken** my new game.
The boys **have cheated** at cards.

5. I took / I have taken
I hid / I have hidden
I grew / I have grown

6. You should have ticked these sentences:
Greg has been to the zoo.
Miles has done lots today.
I have been outside.
We saw the storm.
Helen has come too.
Corrected sentences:
The boys have seen Darren's car.
I have come to visit you.
Izzy has done the dishes.

Page 32 — Staying in the Same Tense

1. You should have circled these words:
take
bought
have
baked

2. You should have circled and corrected these words:
travel — travelled
swim — swam
play — played
fall — fell
leave — left

Punctuation

Section 1 — Sentence Punctuation

Pages 2 and 3 — Capital Letters for Names and I

1. You should have circled:
geoffrey, italy, buckingham palace, april, thursday, mr smith

2. These are the phrases you should have crossed and written out correctly:
25 Church Street
the book by Roald Dahl
the beach in August
Miss Hamilton's class

3. Last weekend, my brother **O**liver went hiking with his friends, **L**ydia and **M**arc. On **S**aturday, they climbed up **S**nowdon, the tallest mountain in **W**ales. Although it rained all day, they said that they had a great time. They want to go again in **S**eptember, but **I** won't go with them because **I** don't enjoy hiking.

4. Luckily, I asked Freida to help me.
Miss Jones said I could be King John in the play.
On Saturday, I watched England play football.
Every June, I go camping in Ireland.

Pages 4 and 5 — Capital Letters and Full Stops

1. These are ham sandwiches**.** Those ones are cheese.
Imran didn't go to school today**.** He was ill.
I love maths**.** I don't like drawing.
My mum's bike is black**.** My dad's is white.

2. The film is very funny.
A mouse ate those sandwiches.
We got lost in the woods

3. We finished the puzzle. It was easy.
It was late. The shops were closing.
My sister loves football. My dad prefers rugby.

4. Any sentence which starts with a capital letter and ends with a full stop. Examples:
My house is in the countryside.
I would really like a cheese sandwich.
We watched the ballet at the theatre.
My uncle drives a blue sports car.

5. Any sentence which starts with a capital letter and ends with a full stop. Examples:
Karl thought the clown was a bit scary.
My cousin has a pet lizard called Larry.
I've played the violin since I was five years old.

Pages 6 and 7 — Question Marks

1. I know who that is — full stop
What colour is your living room — question mark
Do you like reading — question mark
Which way should we go — question mark
I'll go if there's free ice cream — full stop

Punctuation

2. <u>Where</u> did you put my coat?
<u>What</u> is your brother's name?
<u>Why</u> are you telling me off?
<u>How</u> much fruit do you eat?
<u>Who</u> wants to play chess?
<u>When</u> is your birthday?

3. Where are my shoes?
What is the dog called?
Who won the race?
When did she arrive?

4. Any sensible question that is punctuated correctly.
Examples:
What is your name?
When were you born?
Where do you live?

5. Any sentence which starts with a capital letter and ends with a question mark. Examples:
Would you like an apple or a slice of cake?
Do you come to school by bike or by car?
Have you seen the fair in the park?

Pages 8 and 9 — Exclamation Marks

1. We need to hide quickly!
Jim ordered a pizza and some garlic bread.
We've won the lottery!
Just leave your shoes by the door.
Ow, that hurts!
They thought about which film to watch.
There's a shark behind you!

2. You should have ticked:
Give me that now
Watch out
Stop fighting
Catch that thief

3. As soon as Dad stepped through the door, we all jumped out from our hiding places.
"Surprise!" we shouted.
"Blimey!" he exclaimed, putting his hand to his chest, "You nearly gave me a heart attack!"
"Happy birthday, Dad," I said, handing him his present. As he opened it, his eyes grew wide and he grinned.
"It's amazing!" he cried.

4. Any sentence which should end in an exclamation mark. Examples:
"<u>Sit down at once</u>!" the teacher snapped.
"<u>But I really want a pony</u>!" she cried.
"Hurry, Liam, before <u>someone sees us</u>!"
"If we wait any longer <u>we'll miss the show</u>!"
I screamed at the top of my lungs, "<u>Put that down</u>!"

5. Any sentence which starts with a capital letter and ends with an exclamation mark. Example:
I can't believe I won the race!

Pages 10 and 11 — Sentence Practice

1. Come here, right now — exclamation mark
What great news that is — exclamation mark
How do you get to school — question mark
What time is the film on — question mark
I'm playing football tonight — full stop
My mum's name is Rachel — full stop
I really can't believe it — exclamation mark

2. I'm going to Scotland on Friday.
There's a ghost in this house!
When is Matthew's birthday?
Was Catarina born in Portugal?
Mr Baker moved to Australia in May.

3. You've won!
Where are we going?
I'm friends with Ollie.
She crept down the stairs.
Custard is yellow.
Let me go!
Why did you leave?
Ow, that hurts!

4. "I opened my safe," the duke wailed, "and it was gone!"
The detective made a note in her notebook and looked at the duke. He was in his silk pyjamas, gently stroking his pet cat.
"Did anyone else know the code to the safe?" she asked.
"Only my butler," the duke said, "but why would he want to steal Fluffy's diamond collar?"

5. Any sentences which start with a capital letter and end with the correct piece of punctuation. Examples:
Rob is very bored.
Rob is watching the television.
How do we get there?

Section 2 — Commas

Pages 12 and 13 — Writing Lists

1. You should have ticked:
Elena speaks English, Italian, Spanish and French.

2. Nadeem never eats crisps, sweets or chocolate.
Tyler loves to sing, act and dance.
Keira's jumper is red, orange and yellow.

3. Emil needs to buy tomatoes, bananas, carrots and potatoes.

4. Are your eyes green, blue or brown?
The zoo has tigers, lions, zebras and rhinos.
Saskia likes to read, draw, paint and sew.

5. My best friends are Dylan, Zac and Logan. Dylan is funny, friendly and chatty. Zac is very sporty. He likes swimming, cycling and hockey. Logan likes animals. His family have cats, dogs and rabbits. He wants to be a vet when he grows up.

6. Any sentence where commas are used correctly.
   Examples:
   The socks are blue, green, white and spotty.
   The kitten is small, fluffy, ginger and cute.

Pages 14 and 15 — Writing Longer Lists

1. I don't like eating my vegetables, doing my homework, cleaning my bedroom, going to bed early or getting up for school at 7 o'clock.

2. Yosef needs to buy a pint of milk, a bag of apples, a loaf of bread and a tin of baked beans.
   I still need to have a wash, comb my hair, get dressed, eat my breakfast and brush my teeth.
   Mia asked for a red mountain bike, a pair of trainers and a book about dinosaurs.
   I watched a film, helped my mum make lunch, played with my brother and went to my gran's for tea.

3. For this recipe you will need 500 grams of sugar, half a dozen eggs, a kilogram of flour and a spoonful of honey.
   In my beach bag I have a good book, a beach ball, a big towel and a bottle of sun-cream.

4. Any sentence where commas are used correctly.
   Example:
   This weekend I want to go to the beach, build a sand-castle, swim in the sea and eat an ice cream.

Section 3 — Apostrophes

Pages 16 and 17 — Apostrophes for Missing Letters

1. You should have matched these pairs:
   I will — I'll
   she had — she'd
   he is — he's
   they are — they're
   we have — we've

2. was not — wasn't
   it will — it'll
   did not — didn't
   that will — that'll
   where is — where's
   we are — we're

3. You should have put a cross next to these sentences:
   My goats called Susan. (My goat's called Susan.)
   His hamsters got spots. (His hamster's got spots.)
   Her rats got a new cage. (Her rat's got a new cage.)
   Your cats beautiful. (Your cat's beautiful.)
   That rabbits got big ears. (That rabbit's got big ears.)

4. We will
   does not
   She is
   They have

5. They're the best netball team.
   It's raining and I'm getting wet.
   That's the biggest cake I've ever seen.

Pages 18 and 19 — Apostrophes for Single Possession

1. Lucy's teddy bear
   Elena's apple
   Robert's grapes
   Zahra's flower

2. You should have crossed out these phrases:
   the cats
   my sisters'
   her friends

3. You should have ticked:
   Thomas's painting is the best in the class.
   The dress's stripes are blue and purple.

4. The man's house
   The cactus's spikes
   The castle's moat
   The suitcase's handles
   The bus's seats
   The bicycle's wheels
   The keyboard's keys

Pages 20 and 21 — Its and It's

1. You should have ticked:
   Oh no, it's a really hard maths test!
   The bird sang its happy song.
   I practise writing because it's tricky.

2. Do you think (its / it's) far to go?
   The bird flapped (its / it's) wings.
   (Its / It's) great to be on holiday.
   The cat licked (its / it's) fur.
   The rat lost (its / it's) way.
   I cant believe (its / it's) over.
   (Its / It's) a big mess in here.
   The ant carried (its / it's) leaf.

3. My hamster loves ___ ball. — its
   ___ all about taking part. — it's
   Well done, ___ going well. — it's
   The castle opened ___ gates. — its
   ___ been a very long day. — it's
   We should find ___ owner. — its
   ___ been ages since he left. — it's

4. Thank you, it's a lovely present. — it is
   It's been an awful weekend. — it has
   It's taken ages to make this cake. — it has
   I think it's going to snow today. — it is
   I love my jumper because it's warm. — it is
   I wonder if it's time to go home yet? — it is
   It's just begun to snow outside. — it has
   I can't believe it's only 8 o' clock! — it is

Punctuation

Pages 22 and 23 — Apostrophe Practice

1. Your table should look like this:

I am	I'm
you will	you'll
are not	aren't
we had	we'd
does not	doesn't
they have	they've

2. John's
   man's
   moon's
   Maria's

3. You should have ticked:
   You're my best friend.
   She's not very nice to me.
   It's been a great show.
   What's the time, please?

4. You should have added these apostrophes:
   Do you need Sam's help?
   This rug's got a lovely pattern.
   This tin's lid is stuck on tight.
   Your exam's going to be fine.
   That plate's got a stain on it.

5. The door's handle is broken. — to show possession
   My hat's bobbles are pink. — to show possession
   When's the circus coming? — for missing letters
   It's kind to share with others. — for missing letters

6. dog's
   I've
   you'll
   we'd

Section 4 — Inverted Commas

Pages 24 and 25 — Inverted Commas

1. You should have ticked these sentences:
   "Please may I have a sandwich?" asked Ava.
   "Add some salt to the soup," said the chef.

2. You should have added these inverted commas:
   "I've got new spotty wellies," said Nasreen.
   "I'm going to explore the attic next," said Ruby.
   "Art is my favourite subject," said Bryony.
   "My mum's name is Jackie," I said.
   "Mushrooms are slimy and horrible," said Dan.

3. You should have circled these inverted commas:
   "My mum is getting married," said Rosie.
   "When can we go outside?" asked Christopher.
   "We're having a party soon," said Alex.
   "Please can we have pasta for tea?" asked Maya.
   "Be careful with that!" shouted Mrs Wilkins.
   "Are you posting that letter?" asked David.

4. You should have added these inverted commas:
   "Can you give me some advice?" asked Dylan.
   "I'm going to win the race," said Alison.
   "Yes, I'd love to go," replied Matteo.
   "There's a hole in my shoe!" said Kirsty.
   "Let's go and play in the snow," said Luca.

Pages 26 and 27 — Punctuating Speech

1. You should have circled these words:
   this
   you
   no
   excuse
   we

2. You should have ticked these sentences:
   "Have you put your shoes on yet?" I asked.
   Frankie said, "No, I haven't got any more."
   "I bet you can't catch me!" yelled Guy.

3. You should have added these inverted commas and then matched these pairs:
   Ben asked, "is this the way to the circus?" — I
   Emily said, "all the best players practise." — A
   Mikel replied, "yes, I would love to come." — Y
   Henry asked, "do I have to eat my apple?" — D
   Pasha said, "our dad is taking us to the ballet." — O

4. We said, "You can play with us if you don't cheat."
   The queen shouted, "Bring me my crown!"
   The girl asked, "Please may I have a go?"

Pages 28 and 29 — Direct and Reported Speech

1. I asked, "How are we getting there?" — direct speech
   Zack said he's playing rugby later. — reported speech
   "We had a quiet day," Jim told them. — direct speech
   I heard Laura say she would help me. — reported speech
   "I think we should take a break," I said. — direct speech

2. You should have ticked these sentences:
   Are you coming to the playground? asked Flora.
   ("Are you coming to the playground?" asked Flora.)
   Anya said, I've had a great idea for the fair.
   (Anya said, "I've had a great idea for the fair.")

3. direct speech: "Are we there?"
                       "Come here!"
                       "I love you."
   reported speech: Ron asked a question.
                       George says he's tired.
                       Luna talked a lot.

4. You should have added these inverted commas:
   Luke said, "I'm learning to play the piano."
   "Yes, we have lots of crayons in the tin," said Dad.
   "That was the best birthday ever!" I said happily.

Spelling

Section 5 — Paragraphs and Layout

Pages 30 and 31 — Paragraphs

1. You should have ticked these reasons:
   When you're writing about a different time.
   When you're writing about a new place.
   When you're writing about a new person or subject.

2. Paragraphs have to start with 'and'. — false
   Paragraphs have to be two lines long. — false
   A new paragraph starts on a new line. — true
   Paragraphs are groups of sentences. — true
   Only use paragraphs when you want to. — false

3. person
   time
   subject

4. You should have added these three paragraph markers:
   A few months ago, Harriet's mum took her to visit the zoo. She saw lions and tigers, as well as monkeys and bears. Harriet thought it was amazing. // The next weekend Harriet found out that the zoo wanted some school-children to start working at the zoo. She signed up straight away. // Now Harriet goes along to the zoo every Saturday morning. She feeds the animals and helps to look after them. // Next month, Harriet is going to be there when the new baby penguins are born. She can't wait!

Page 32 — Headings and Subheadings

1. You should have ticked these statements:
   A heading tells you the main subject of the text.
   Subheadings break up a text into smaller sections.

2. You should have matched these pairs:
   Fish and chips — Deep-fried fish served with chips. Usually served as take-away food with salt and vinegar.
   Sticky Toffee Pudding — A steamed pudding made with sponge, dates and toffee sauce. Often served with custard.
   English Breakfast — Eggs, bacon, sausages, beans and toast. Often served all day — not just for breakfast.

Spelling
Section 1 — Prefixes

Pages 2 and 3 — Prefixes — 'un' 'dis' and 'mis'

1. **un + known, mis + print, dis + approve, un + even**
2. **unaware, unequal, disregard, unpaid, misbehave**
3. You should have underlined: **diskind, discalculate, unspell** and **misappoint**.
   The correct spellings are: **unkind, miscalculate, misspell** and **disappoint**.
4. **disown, mistreat, mismatch, dismiss, displease, disagree**
5. **un**well, **un**locked, **dis**appeared, **mis**understood, **un**packed

Page 4 — Prefixes — 're' and 'anti'

1. **anti**clockwise, **anti**septic, **re**charge, **re**fresh, **re**write, **anti**climax, **re**create, **re**heat, **re**design
2. **reapply, antibiotic, reopen, antivirus, resend, return**

Page 5 — Prefixes — 'sub' and 'super'

1. **submarine, superglue, supermarket, subdivided**
2. **sub**merge, **super**sonic, **super**man, **sub**heading
3. Any correctly spelt words that start with the correct prefixes.
   Examples:
   superhero, supersize, superpower, superstar sublet, sublevel, submerge, subtotal, subtitles

Section 2 — Suffixes and Word Endings

Pages 6 and 7 — Suffixes — 'ing' and 'ed'

1. **hunting, hunted**
   jumping, jumped
   treating, treated
2. peform**ing**, entertain**ed**, deliver**ing**
3. **enjoyed, shopping, struggling, employed, carried, stopped, celebrating**
4. You should have underlined: **worryed, balanceing, puzzleing, hurryed, cryed**.
   The correct spellings are: **worried, balancing, puzzling, hurried, cried**.

Pages 8 and 9 — Suffixes — 'er' and 'est'

1. **older, fewer, smaller, taller, oldest, fewest, smallest, tallest**
2. cold**er**, cold**est**, fast**est**, rich**er**
3. sing**er**, gardene**r**, teach**er**, bank**er**, plumb**er**, wait**er**
4. **nastier, voter, spicier, tiniest, dancer, buyer, fatter, easiest**
5. You should have circled: **funnyest, manageer, shinyer, bikeers, muddyest**.
   The correct spellings are: **funniest, manager, shinier, bikers, muddiest**.

Pages 10 and 11 — Suffixes — 'ment' 'ness' 'ful' and 'less'

1. **fearful, sadness, enjoyment, stressful, playful**
2. **spotless, equipment, brightness**
3. **beautiful, penniless, laziness, merciful, happiness, bumpiness, merriment**
4. mercy — **merciless**, easy — **easiness**, hope — **hopeless**, care — **careful**, arrange — **arrangement**

Spelling

Pages 12 and 13 — Suffixes — 'ation' and 'ous'

1. **plantation, famous, publication**
2. You should have underlined: **celebrateion, locateation, glamourous**
   The correct spellings are: **celebration, location, glamorous**
3. **preparation, invitation, outrageous**
4. mountain**ous**, danger**ous**, inform**ation**, hazard**ous**, expect**ation**
5. Across: 1. **courageous** 2. **poisonous**
   Down: 1. **glamorous** 2. **infectious**

Pages 14 and 15 — Suffixes — 'ly'

1. **angrily, rudely, simply, gently**
2. **deadly, busily, frantically, gladly, nobly**
3. You should have ticked: **boldly, badly, softly, calmly, meanly.**
   You should have crossed: **cuddlely, sensiblely, humblely, subtlely.**
   The correct spellings are: cudd**ly**, sensib**ly**, humb**ly**, subt**ly**.
4. **warmly, slightly, ably**
5. Any words ending in -ly that are spelt correctly.
   Examples:
   smoothly, quietly, loudly, proudly

Pages 16 and 17 — Word Endings — 'sure' and 'ture'

1. **picture, measure, gesture, nature, pleasure**
2. **enclosure, manufacture, composure, mixture, structure, treasure**
3. **leisure, torture, creature**
4. **treasure, furniture, temperature, composure, adventure**
5. Any words ending in -sure or -ture that are spelt correctly.
   Examples:
   closure, unsure, assure, ensure, pressure, reassure capture, feature, posture, nurture, culture

Section 3 — Confusing Words

Page 18 — The Short 'i' Sound

1. Words with a short 'i' sound: **spill, gym, rapid, syrup**
   Words with a long 'i' sound: **nice, pine, wire, wife**
2. **wish, tiger, chin, time, crypt**
3. in**s**ect, panic, gift, crystal, syrup, mystery, satisfy, since

Page 19 — The Hard 'c' Sound

1. atta**ck**, walking, **c**offee, **k**itten, cri**ck**et, do**c**tor
2. **castle, duck**
3. homesi**ck**, o**c**topus, s**k**eleton

Page 20 — The Soft 'c' Sound

1. **sentence, space, excited, pencil**
2. **grace, absent, justice, icy, cancel, insist**
3. sen**c**e, a**c**id, dan**c**e, spi**c**y, de**c**ent, house, chase, upset

Page 21 — The 'sh' Sound

1. **sh**oe, parachute, sugar, **sh**ark
2. **machine, tissue, shampoo, brochure**
3. **ashamed, pressure**

Page 22 — The 'ay' Sound

1. **afraid, brave, anyway, essay**
2. **sailor, grapes, calculate**
3.

Page 23 — Word Families

1. **defrost, frosting, frostbite, frosted**
2. face, preface: **surface, deface, facing, facial**
   itself, herself: **selfish, himself, selfless, myself**
3. Any correctly spelt words from the correct word family.
   Examples:
   taking, retake
   dated, outdated
   doing, undo

Pages 24 and 25 — Plurals

1. church**es**, piano**s**, key**s**, potato**es**, box**es**
2. pon**ies**, lea**ves**, difficult**ies**, shop**s**, torch**es**, bucket**s**, wol**ves**, thie**ves**, apolog**ies**, shel**ves**, fox**es**, pencils
3. **geese, mice, reflexes, elves, women**
4. **teeth, halves, cliffs**
5. Any sentence containing the correct plural.
   Examples:
   The **donkeys** were tired after their long journey.
   We had ham **sandwiches** for lunch.
   I baked three **batches** of cookies.

Spelling

Pages 26 and 27 — Possessive Apostrophes

1. You should have crossed: **Gemmas' bat, Amy's kitten's, Jeremys' pens**
   The correct phrases are: Gemma**'s** bat, Amy's kittens, Jeremy**'s** pens

2. You should have underlined: **Judiths, Mums, Matts, Jackies, Kevins**
   The correct spellings are: Judith's, Mum's, Matt's, Jackie's, Kevin's.

3. **It's** your turn to do the washing-up.
   The gorilla beat **its** chest to scare **its** rival.
   Mrs Kirk's cat ate all of **its** food straight away.

4. The bride's veil, the pirate's ship, the soldier's uniform, the cleaner's mop

5. Any sentences that use possessive apostrophes correctly.
   Examples:
   My grandma's name is Jeanne.
   Thomas's football kit was very dirty.
   The parrot's claws were very sharp.

Pages 28 and 29 — Homophones

1. **mane, bee, bear, sun**

2. Vegetarians don't eat **meat**.
   Where shall we **meet**?
   I can't **accept** this.
   I like all vegetables **except** carrots.
   Don't **break** anything.
   Make sure you **brake** at the corner.

3. Becky and Amber dyed **their** hair the same colour.
   Are **there** any biscuits left in the tin?
   Three people said **they're** coming to my party.

4. You should have written: **rain, hear, deer, made**

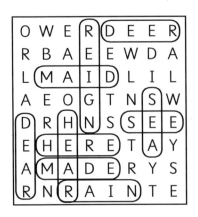

5. Any sentence where the word is used correctly.
   Examples:
   I am going **to** Oxford.
   There are **two** sides to the argument.
   I like that one **too**.

Section 4 — Mixed Practice

Pages 30 to 32 — Mixed Practice

1. **un + paid, sub + category, mis + trust, re + cycle**

2. **busier, busiest, busying, busied**
   happiest, happily, happier, happiness

3. You should have circled: **merryment, usualy, disimilar, angryly, picsure,**
   The correct spellings are: **merriment, usually, dissimilar, angrily, picture,**

4. ba**ck**, i**ce**, s**k**etch, fan**cy**, **c**ook, absent

5. **mystery, chalet, weight, machine, They, myth**

6. **countries, boxes, thieves, potatoes**

7. You should have crossed: **Andys' hat, Ruths' mug, Lily's cat's**

8. Across clues: 1. **neck** 2. **misbehave** 3. **once** 4. **tricks**
   Down clues: 1. **neighbour** 2. **subway**

9. Any sentence where the words are used correctly.
   Examples:
   I went to a **sale** and bought a **sail**.
   I have a problem with my left **eye**.

Chew longer for a fuller flavour

ISBN 978 1 78294 150 7
9 781782 941507

CGP

E3SA21   £2.00
(Retail Price)

www.cgpbooks.co.uk

© CGP — 2014